I wish...

DREAMS AND REALITIES
OF
PARENTING A SPECIAL NEEDS CHILD

Kate Divine McAnaney

Editions DSG
Special Needs Project
Good Books about Disabilities
3463 State Street, Suite 282
Santa Barbara, CA 93105

Editions DSG™ is an imprint of
Special Needs Project

I Wish...
Dreams and Realities of Parenting a Special Needs Child
Second expanded edition 1998

Cover design by Laurel Burch

ISBN 0-9655138-4-X

I Wish...Dreams and Realities of Parenting a Special Needs Child
was originally published by the United Cerebral Palsy Association
of California in 1992

Editions DSG books are available for quantity purchase by
schools and agencies, and for special promotions. For details
contact Director, Special Markets.

To my Family

Patrick
for your loving support, encouragement
and invaluable editorial assistance

Mahlon and Michael
for your love and patience
as I keep learning about parenting

Bob and Irm, Evelyn and Elmer
for being such outstanding grandparents
to my children

And to my larger family
of special friends and relatives
–you know who you are–
for being there when I need you.

Special thanks to Lauren Burch for believing in
this project and donating the incredible cover art.

I wish...
TABLE OF CONTENTS

Foreword

Part I: Parenting a child with special needs

I wish I could...

...figure out why this happened to me!................................1

...turn back the clock and make it all turn out differently. 3

...get off this emotional roller coaster!................................5

...stop feeling guilty about my child's condition.....................7

...find a teacher or social worker who would take a personal interest in my child's progress 9

...see the world from my child's eyes for just one day...........11

...relax and not feel so compelled to stay on top of every new treatment, therapy or cure. 13

...get over this grief once and for all...................................15

...find a friend who really understands what my life is like. ...17

...realize that I'm the best mom for this child 19

    Erma Bombeck: "God does work in mysterious ways"..21

...disappear and not be anybody's 'mom' today 22

...get a whole night's sleep! 23

...have a peek into the future to see if my child will be okay as an adult...25

...be more trusting!...27

...not be so obsessed with my child's disability 29

...get the professionals to their jobs more effectively 31

...learn to have more patience 33

...maintain a positive attitude with the professionals 35

...be a better advocate for my child 37

    Effective Parent Advocacy: The Four P's 39

...feel more free and supported by all this assistance I'm
    getting 40

...keep other people from offering advice 41

...get a break from making all these decisions! 43

...figure out if I'm a wonder-woman or a wimp 45

...separate my child from his disability for a day. 47

...sleep in on Sunday mornings 49

...get other people to treat my child like a real person. 51

...figure out if mainstreaming is the right placement 53

    Successful Mainstreaming 55

...know if I'm doing too much for my child 56

...find equipment that meets all of our needs 57

...know how having a disabled sibling is affecting my other
    child 59

..make things perfect for my child all the time 61

...make my life easier! 63

    Poem: "Signature on this line, please" 65

Part II: Looking back: Messages from disabled adults

I wish...

...my mom knew how much I truly love her for pushing me
to be all that I can be 67
Mike Kinter

...I wish... 70
Craig Clifton

...I could tell the world, "Let me be me.".............................71
Millicent Rogers

...I could always have my physical independence. 73
Amber del Vito

...I could empower more disabled people. 77
Randy Kitch

...people didn't think of me as disabled............................79
Marty Clayman, MD

...that more parents of disabled children recognized that
feeding the soul is just as important
as treating the body. 81
Kathleen Lankasky.

References...87

FOREWORD

My son Mahlon - arriving two months prematurely and weighing less than three pounds - has changed my life. He redefined parenting for me by giving me experiences and opportunities I never expected. Physically challenged by cerebral palsy, Mahlon has often been a source of inspiration to me. His insight, his endurance, and his *courage* continue to surprise me and to lift my spirits.

Many times in my years as the parent of a child with special needs, I have needed a word of encouragement or a gentle nudge to help me find a different perspective on a situation. Conversations with other special parents have taught me that I am not alone in this need. I have also learned that these parents are some of the most creative and most adaptable of parents!

With *I Wish...* I want to offer you some encouraging words, some inspiration, some understanding. I hope this book comes to you at the right time and that sharing it with others will help people know what special needs parenting is all about.

A radiance of good wishes to you and your family.

Kate Divine McAnaney

Part I:

Parenting a child with special needs

❖   ❖   ❖

I wish...

I could figure out why this happened to me!

In active labor at six and a half months, I was well on the way to delivering a premature baby. I knew the baby would be low-birth-weight and would be at-risk. The doctor also said the baby might die and if he survived, he might have disabilities. I wanted to scream out loud: "I didn't plan *this!* I planned to have a normal baby! What am I going to do? This shouldn't be happening... to *me!*"

I did a quick review of the pregnancy, searching for some reason: Was I too active? Was I too inactive? Was it something I ate or drank? I cast back frantically through my life to see if I'd done something to 'deserve' this. I found no answers.

'How' it happened may eventually be discovered, but the question that's been asked by millions before, *Why me?*, goes unanswered. What a time of mixed emotions! You feel such a sense of loss for not having the 'perfect' baby you expected, and yet, at the same time, you cannot reject this little person that's yours.

Mourning for the things your child *isn't* is normal. You *should* grieve at shattered expectations. It's a healthy way to begin recognizing and accepting your child for who he or she *is.*

You might want to turn the *Why me* question around and ask *Why not me?* I've found that I'm far more patient, far more resourceful, and far stronger (emotionally and physically) than I ever would have given myself credit for when my son Mahlon was first born. When I shifted my focus from the shattered dreams to the unexpected *opportunities* this kind of mothering would reveal, I really began to handle it.

Today, I will remember that even though this situation is unfair, I am capable of handling it.

"There is no such thing as a problem without a gift for you in its hands."

Richard Bach
Illusions

I wish...

I could turn back the clock and make it all turn out differently.

"If only I could go back to the time a few weeks before I delivered my son and put myself on complete bedrest. Maybe then I could have prevented the premature labor!" This was a familiar refrain from me for the first years of Mahlon's life. I desperately wanted a chance to do it all over and create a different ending. Now, so many years later, when I try to imagine my life without this special needs child, I'm not so sure I would choose a different life. Of course I will always wish that Mahlon didn't have cerebral palsy for his sake, but compared to this life, a 'normal' life might seem boring.

I wasn't trained for this kind of mothering; I wasn't expecting it, and my son didn't come with an instruction manual on how to best handle his special needs for optimum functioning, but our family has managed. We have learned and grown and changed. And I can recognize now that even though this is a different kind of mothering than I'd planned on, maybe, it's different 'good' and not different 'bad'. I'm still a Mom. I'm still needed. And I have the opportunity to make a difference in the world by teaching people how to accept children with special needs. I also have the opportunity to see the world from the unique perspective of an individual with disabilities.

Today, I will remember that 'normal' isn't necessarily better.

"Life's most painful losses can lead to life's most beautiful findings."

Rusty Berkus
Appearances

I wish...
I could get off this emotional roller coaster!

Exceptional parenting is almost always unexpected. It is often frustrating and it is continuously challenging. It creates inner turmoil with intense emotions always threatening to break through to the surface. Anger, denial, resentment, confusion and fear are interspersed with brief intervals of joy, pride, triumph, or relief.

Yet just when you begin to think that you have everything under control, the universe springs another surprise on you. An event, an illness, an equipment failure, or a new bureaucratic difficulty tips the balance and you are plunged back into the emotional whirlpool.

When this happens to me, (and yes, it still happens, even after 15 years), I realize that no one has the power to maintain rigid control over every aspect of life. It takes tremendous energy to keep the lid on my emotional pressure-cooker.

Sometimes the lid has to come off! It is appropriate to be angry when your child suffers needlessly, or is not receiving services. It's natural to feel resentment when you can't get the assistance you need from a spouse, agency, or professional. It is normal to experience grief when a new situation arises that defines your child's limitations. But these emotional states are not permanent. Once negative emotion is released, you can take the next neccesary step for your child in a more productive state of mind.

Today, I will remember that strong emotions are part of the job of parenting. I will not waste energy trying to deny them or hold them back. I will feel them, release them, and get back to the task at hand.

"Tough times never last, tough people do."

Unknown

I wish...
I could stop feeling guilty about my child's condition.

I still remember how insulted I felt when the doctor told me that my early labor and premature delivery was due to an 'incompetent cervix'. I realize now that the ridiculous term only describes a medical abnormality, but it sounded like a personal affront! I had, up until then, felt very confident about my ability to control most areas of my life. I was like the woman in the Anne Murray song: "I'm strong, I'm sure, I'm in control; a lady with a plan...".

I certainly never anticipated that I would have any problem having babies. "How could I *fail* at such a basic task?" I asked myself. I felt cheated! It was like I had failed a test that no one had told me to study for. And the end result had directly affected my child!

There was an appalling sense of guilt that came rushing in with that casual diagnosis the doctor gave me. For him it was an enlightening discovery, an answer to a riddle. For me it was a crushing revelation.

My first son had been born very prematurely and he lived only a few hours. Doctors at that time told me it was 'just a fluke', but when I went into premature labor in my second pregnancy, we knew there was something wrong with me that had made it happen. As my miniature second son struggled with respirators and IV's, I struggled with my guilt and embarrassment at having 'created' such a challenge for so small and so dear a person. I stroked his tiny hand as he lay hooked up to all that equipment. And I pumped breast milk so that he could have it when he was ready to drink. And I cried and I prayed that both of us would make it out of that intensive care nursery and be 'okay'. We did make it and we're okay. The old guilt will probably always be there, a faint shadow that sometimes sneaks up on me when I'm especially tired or vulnerable.

I berated myself for so many years saying: "If only I'd known.. I would have taken it easier... I would have been more conscientious...I would have insisted the doctor check me more often..." But I wasn't as assertive then as I am now and I didn't have enough information to make any different choices. I have to accept that I did my best, at that time.

Today, I will remember that even though I can't completely erase the remembered pain of feeling responsible for my child's condition, I *can* forgive myself for any real or imagined failures. I can offer *myself* the same unconditional love my child offers me.

"Have patience with all things, but first of all with yourself."

Frances de Sales

I wish...

I could find a teacher or social worker who would take a personal interest in my child's progress so that I wouldn't have to try so hard to get all the information.

When my son first entered an Infant Stimulation Program, I was thrilled and relieved to have some assistance in planning activities and setting goals for him. Most of the other children in our Mom and Baby group were more 'involved' than my son and nearly all were non-verbal. But I was confident that each of us was getting the best planning for our child and that we were where we belonged.

At the beginning of our second year in the program, I happened to hear about a class that seemed more appropriate for my son. It was also a county program, but it was specifically designed for orthopedically handicapped children who were capable of participating in a regular curriculum. It was in a school that was only a few miles from our home. I was surprised that no one at the Infant Stim Program had told me about it.

When I asked, I was astonished to learn from the teachers that they were hoping to keep Mahlon in their program because he verbally stimulated the other children! I had trusted them with my son's progress and it hurt to realize that *his* best interests had been overlooked. It was an enlightening experience that taught me not to *assume* that the 'professionals' have all the right answers.

Today, I will remember that I will always have to work *with* the professionals involved in my child's education and therapy and that together we can determine what is right.

"I forgive myself and everyone else for not being perfect."

Kate McAnaney

I wish...

I could see the world from my child's eyes for just one day to know that he or she is okay in his or her own way.

I remember when my son was eight months old and all my friends' babies of that age were energetically crawling around the room, getting themselves to things that interested them. I agonized for my son as I watched him energetically, but ineffectively wriggle around trying to get where he wanted to go. It hurt me to see him try so hard to accomplish so little. Then one day, putting my own misery aside, I noticed that *he* seemed happy! He had a goal, he was putting his energy toward that goal and, if I gently assisted by placing objects within reasonable reach, he could achieve his goal.

It was then that I realized that he may not be as frustrated as I by his limitations! His way of doing things was okay with him. As he has grown older, he does sometimes lament that he can't do something, but grieving over abilities he's *never* had is not a long-held grief. He continues to discover his own way of doing things, asks for help when he needs it, and goes about his own business. That reminds me of when Santa asked Mahlon once, "Have you been a good little boy?" and Mahlon quipped brightly, "I've been good enough!"

Today, I will remember that my perspective is different from my child's. I'll remember not to get caught up in grieving on his behalf. I will focus on what my child *can* do and will help him set reasonable goals.

"The world is filled with people who have been handed life's 'worst' and they have become winners."

Susan Jeffers, PhD
Feel the Fear and Do It Anyway

I wish...

I could relax and not feel so compelled to stay on top of every new treatment, therapy, medication or cure.

I'm a devoted fan of miracle-cure stories (I love happy endings). Since my son was born, I've been on the lookout for new and better therapies, surgery techniques, or medical equipment. We live in an area where the New Age culture flourishes and occasionally I'm approached by someone who practices some new massage technique, or holistic healing regimen which they feel will surely 'cure' Mahlon's cerebral palsy.

A part of me is always hopeful when I encounter such alternative healers, or read about new treatments or see ads for products that might at long last be the elusive cure. I've learned that traditional medical science does not have all the answers. If it did, my son and I wouldn't have to continue this quest for new and more satisfactory forms of healing.

Yet after all these years I've become a bit jaded. Energy is a valuable commodity in my life and my energy is important to my family. I have to weigh the costs in time, emotion, and possibility of failure. Sometimes the costs of experimenting are too high.

My son is old enough now, that I let *him* choose who's going to work on him. We'll keep trying new techniques and approaches, and we'll never stop hoping. But we can't try *everything* so the process of choosing new therapy has become more selective over the years.

Today, I will remember to take a moment to *relax*

with my child. We will go to the park, read a story or just hold each other. It takes too much energy to think about 'fixing' my child all the time. And it leaves me with less energy to enjoy him. If a true miracle arises I trust that we will hear about it. When it comes we will be ready. But for today, *I love my son as he is.*

"Life is a classroom where it's okay to ask questions and if you don't get all the answers, you pass anyway."
Rusty Berkus
Appearances

I wish...
I could get over this grief once and for all!

When you lose someone close to you, or when you have a miscarriage, or when you have a child with special needs, you experience grief. At first you're in shock, then you try to make it go away (this can't be happening to me!), then come anger, guilt, and depression, but not in any set order. Then you are 'supposed to' reach resolution or acceptance. People expect you to grieve and get over it. In some situations it works that way. But when you have a child with a disability, the grief process is on-going; it's never fully resolved because the disability is always there and you have to deal with it everyday.

The *chronic grief* you feel as the parent of a special needs child is not debilitating. It's usually a quiet whisper in the back of your mind. But when you face a new crisis with your child or are worn down from battling with service providers, it will *scream* out at you. And there you'll be, back in shock, anger, guilt or depression.

According to Judy Tatelbaum, grief counselor, "Only in fairy tales does the hero slay the dragon once and for all, and live happily ever after. In real life, the dragons keep coming. Considering the dragons we will probably have to slay in a lifetime - we need tools for handling our inevitable encounters with life."

The trick to *managing* chronic grief is accepting it as a part of your life, and acknowledging that any 'flares-ups' are appropriate and are *temporary*. You *can* and will get back on top of things when the crisis passes or when you take some time out to rest and to nurture *yourself*.

Today, I will forgive myself for an occasional lapse into grief. I'll credit myself with all the situations I've managed successfully (or just survived). I will realize that I *am* okay.

"Grief is a natural and healthy response to loss, disappointment and change."

Judy Tatelbaum
You Don't Have To Suffer

I wish...
I could find a friend who really understands what my life is like.

When my son was born, all my girlfriends were having babies too. We were all able to stay home with our children and enjoyed getting together for picnics at the park. As our children grew, it became increasingly discouraging and depressing to see *my* child's limitations.

I couldn't sit and chat at the park like the other mothers. My son needed assistance to swing or slide or play in the sand box. I was determined that he was not going to miss out on anything that was interesting to kids his age. I loved being part of this group and the other moms were very supportive, but they didn't really know what it was like to be in my situation.

I belonged to another group of moms also and from them came the reassurance that I was going to be okay. We were the mothers of all the babies and toddlers in the Infant Stimulation Program. We would have our coffee-and-chat break during the time our kids were in program. Here I could let it all hang out. We talked about resentment at mismanaged pregnancies and birthings; frustration with case managers who didn't manage, doctors who didn't listen, and spouses who didn't help.

This was a safe place to express my feelings where the listener would really understand and wouldn't think I was 'falling apart' or 'still grieving' or 'not handling it too well'. We laughed together. We cried together. Even though our children had different disabilities, we were alike: Alike in our anger; alike in our fear; alike in our hope. I found I needed both groups of women in order to maintain the balance I wanted in my life and to maintain, what I felt, was a tenuous sanity.

Today, I will make contact with another special needs parent through a letter, a phone call, a visit. Or I will write a letter to Family Forum in *Exceptional Parent* Magazine and try to make a connection with another mom in my situation.

"There is a destiny that makes us brothers,
No one goes his way alone.
All that we send into the lives of others,
Comes back again into our own."
Edwin Markham

I wish...

I could realize that I'm the best mom for this child and stop focusing on my inadequacies.

Now that I'm the parent of teenagers, I have to face the fact that even if I had an impeccable self-image and even if I had extraordinary confidence in my ability to parent, my darling adolescents would conjure up inadequacies *for* me! I don't think any parent escapes adolescent scrutiny without some 'flaws'. We'd all like to be perfect parents but we each have a unique set of circumstances, and we can just do our best within that framework. My best will be different from your best just as my parenting experience is different from yours.

When you have a child with special needs in the family, there are so many outside *authorities* involved in your life (doctors, therapists, special education directors, financial assistance counselors...) that it's easy to be tricked into thinking that you're not measuring up as a parent. There's always someone who will subtly imply or bluntly state that you could be and should be doing *more*... more therapy, more behavior modification, more homework. The truth is, they are usually only looking at a small *part* of your life. You are living your life, not them. You have the whole picture and you must decide what works for you and your family.

You have to shield yourself from unwarranted criticism and unwanted suggestions. Once upon a time I would agree with critical input saying "Yes, you're right! God really made a mistake when he gave me this child!" But now I take a deep breath, restrain my defensive reaction and simply respond: "I'm doing my best you know. I realize you might act differently if you were in my shoes, but you're *not* in my shoes." This will help re-orient the 'authority' on who's really in charge of the situation. It will give you back your personal power and will keep you from focusing on real or imagined inadequacies.

We do have to keep trying to meet our children's needs. We can't just cave-in and ignore our obligations, but we have to recognize that we have limitations.. on our time, on our energy, on our initiative. The *best* we can do for our children is to love them and to love ourselves.

Today, I will remember that everyone brings their own experience to parenting. I will recognize that I have the opportunity to develop new strengths and to overcome what I feel are weaknesses. I love my children and they love me and what others think scarcely matters.

"Argue for your limitations and sure enough they're yours."

Richard Bach
Illusions

God does work in mysterious ways.

Most women become mothers by accident, some by choice, a few by social pressures and a couple by habit.

This year, nearly 100,000 women will become mothers of handicapped children. Did you ever wonder how mothers of handicapped children are chosen?

Somehow I visualize God hovering over earth selecting His instruments for propagation with great care and deliberation. As He observes, He instructs His angels to make notes in a giant ledger.

"Armstrong, Beth, son, Patron saint, Matthew. Forrest, Marjorie, daughter, patron saint, Cecelia."

"Rutledge, Carrie, twins, patron saint... give her Gerard. He's used to profanity."

Finally, He passes a name to an angel and smiles, "Give her a handicapped child."

The angel is curious. "Why this one, God? She's so happy."

"Exactly," smiles God. "Could I give a handicapped child a mother who does not know laughter? That would be cruel."

"But has she patience?" asks the angel.

"I don't want her to have too much patience or she will drown in a sea of self-pity and despair. Once the shock and resentment wears off, she'll handle it.

"I watched her today. She has that feeling of self and independence in a mother. You see, the child I'm going to give her has his own world. She has to make it live in her world and that's not going to be easy."

"But, Lord, I don't think she even believes in you."

God smiles. "No matter. I can fix that. This one is perfect. She has just enough selfishness."

The Angel gasps, "Selfishness? Is that a virtue?"

God nods. "If she can't separate herself from her child occasionally, she'll never survive. Yes, here is a woman whom I will bless with a child less than perfect. She doesn't realize it yet, but she is to be envied. She will never take for granted a 'spoken word'. She will never consider a 'step' ordinary. When her child says 'Momma' for the first time she will be present at a miracle and know it! When she describes a tree or a sunset to her blind child, she will see it as a few people ever see my creations.

"I will permit her to see clearly the things I see... ignorance, cruelty, prejudice...and allow her to rise above them all. She will never be alone, I will be at her side every minute of every day of her life because she is doing my work as surely as she is here by my side."

"And what about her patron saint?" asks the angel, his pen poised in mid-air.

God smiles. "A mirror will suffice."

ERMA BOMBECK
"At Wit's End"

I wish...

I could disappear and not be anybody's Mom today. It's too much to deal with. I can't handle all this!

I used to live in a home that had one large upstairs room, away from the rest of the house. I used it as my bedroom. When my children were toddlers and I was a frazzled single parent, I would sometimes retreat to my 'tower' and pretend that I had no responsibilities other than to amuse myself with a good book or a soothing tape. The respite usually didn't last more than a half hour and it was never enough, but it helped me break the 'martyr' pattern of thinking that I was required to live and breathe only for my children.

In those brief moments of quiet reflection I could renew my sense of self and remember that *I* was important too; that I was Kate, a person, with lots of abilities and interests that did not all coincide with my role as Mommy. I came to realize that a little selfishness is not a bad thing. If I could enjoy myself more, I could enjoy my children more.

Today, I will remember that my needs are important too and if I focus only on my child's needs that I will end up depriving us both. I will plan some time off from the role of Mom.

"All this healing, loving, giving and caring is just like breathing: You can't just breathe out, you have to bring it in for yourself also."

Patrick McAnaney

22

I wish...

I could get a whole night's sleep. I start every day with less than enough sleep! It's draining me.

If I were to choose one word to characterize myself as a parent of a disabled child, one word to sum up my experience, I would have to choose 'tired'. It's a tiredness that is sometimes beyond respite care relief. It's from too many nights of interrupted sleep and too many demands on my physical, emotional, and mental energy.

I'm tired of having to deal with professionals who are insensitive to my situation. I'm tired of trying to convince service providers that I really need a piece of equipment. I'm tired of coaxing agencies to move the paperwork along more quickly. And I'm tired of hearing a little voice call "Maaahm!" in the middle of the night. I sometimes feel like I'm drawing on an empty tank; and that I will soon come to an abrupt standstill. But I know that I'll keep going, because I *have to* keep going. And when the teacher calls, or the social worker calls, I want to say "Don't think I'm disinterested in my child or that I'm shirking my responsibility, *sometimes I'm just tired.*"

Sleep is important, as many sleep-deprivation studies have shown. It's a time for re-fueling physical and emotional energy and it's an essential part of *everyone's* life.

Today, I will remember that it's okay to take a break from my life even if it means getting a babysitter so that I can take an *uninterrupted* bath or nap!

"Do you love yourself enough to ask for what you need?"

Rusty Berkus
Appearances

I wish...

I could have a peek into the future to see if my child will be okay as an adult...Who will care for him? Who will advocate for him? Who will love him?

I've found that I can't handle too much of the future in the present time. I do worry and wonder what it will be like for Mahlon as an adult, but if I project myself too far ahead and borrow 'challenges' from tomorrow, I won't have enough energy to get through today's challenges! I've learned to be an energy conservationist and to avoid unnecessary stress.

When my son was a preschooler, people would ask, "What will you do when he's in elementary school?" When he was in elementary, people wondered what I would do about the pressures of junior high. Now that he's nearing the end of eighth grade, the question is "What will happen in high school? Will he go to college?" My answer has always been, "I'll deal with that when I get to it." I really don't know what answers I'll have for tomorrow's questions. I know there will always be problems to solve and there *will be* solutions to be found. So even though I do worry about his future, I don't dwell on it.

I've done what I can to safeguard my children - there's life insurance and I've selected a guardian and I keep all Mahlon's various paperwork in order. While I'm still around I know that I will continue to accept the challenges that require my input and will hopefully know when the challenge belongs to my son and not to me.

Today, I will remember that all mothers worry about their children's futures; about whether their children will find loving mates, satisfying jobs, adequate housing. I will focus on the present and won't overwhelm myself with future concerns.

"The best thing about the future is that it comes only one day at a time."

Abraham Lincoln

I wish...
I could be more trusting.

It's hard to be trusting when you feel you have to be on constant guard against incompetence. Of course, not everyone who works with your child is incompetent, but those who are need to be corrected and supervised.

I think my wariness began during the long days when my premature son was in the Neonatal Intensive Care Unit. Watchfulness became a habit. My son was in a room full of critically ill infants and I felt I had to stay alert in case the staff missed something with *my* baby. Even the best of staffs don't see everything. One time the suctioning tube had been left on and as my son wriggled around, the tube 'attached' itself to his tiny arm. It had sucked a nice blood blister to the surface before I noticed it and called the nurse. This was an insignificant event for the nurse, but it powerfully affected me!

I learned to watch the dials on the machinery; to watch my son's intakes and outputs; and to watch the doctors and nurses watch my son. Somewhere in the intensity of all that, my assertiveness was born and 'eternal vigilance' became a way of life. I started to ask questions: "What is this procedure for? Are you sure he's supposed to look like this? Who *are* you and what are you doing to my baby?"

I have continued to ask questions over the years. I view it as 'informed parenting' rather than paranoid distrust! Professionals should be able and willing to answer questions and if they are too impatient or too annoyed with my asking, then I don't care to have them working with my child.

Today, I will remember that asking questions is the mark of a concerned parent. I learn from the answers and my questions contribute to the effectiveness of the professionals.

"Learning to trust is one of life's most difficult tasks."
Issac Watts

I wish...

I were not so obsessed with my child's disability.

Parenting a special needs child takes so much thinking and planning, scheduling and *doing* that it's easy to lose our*selves* in the whirlwind of activity. It's important to take a moment to remember who you were before you had this child. What did you like to do? Play tennis; read; swim; walk; write? You'll be a better balanced and happier mommy if you set aside time for yourself; time to do the things you like.

I came to this conclusion when I was single parenting my sons. I hated asking for help, but finally realized that being a stressed-out Martyr-Mom was not the best I could give my children. After I began asking for help, a remarkable thing happened: I sensed that I was *giving* as well as receiving a gift. I was allowing people to help me and it made *them* feel good. They figured out unique ways to entertain Mahlon, to position him, to transport him and to adapt games for him and I benefitted from their discoveries. They enriched my life and my children enriched theirs.

I found out there were county and state agencies that could offer 'respite care' or could subsidize child care costs. At first I would only use their services for necessary things like appointments or grocery shopping. But after some enlightening counselling sessions, I gave myself permission to have some personal pleasure. I got to where I felt comfortable using babysitters so I could go to a movie, take an aerobics class, or go out to lunch with friends. I learned to be more *self*-nurturing and as a result, nurturing my children was less stressful and more fun.

Today, I will make a list of the things that I like to do and I will do at least one of those things this week.

"One of the bonuses about loving yourself is that you get to feel good."

Louise Hay
Healing Thoughts

I wish...

*I could get the professionals to do their jobs more
effectively so that I could just be a mom!*

When you're feeling overwhelmed with meeting all
your child's needs and meeting all the other
obligations in your family, it's natural to wish for
Rescue. You long for that case manager extraordinaire
who will do everything so effectively and so efficiently
that all you'll have to do is sit and rock your baby; take
him on walks and sing him lullabies. But face it, the
White Knight isn't coming, and if he did we'd probably
have to clean up after the horse in addition to rocking
the baby.

It's frustrating, it's annoying and it's *unfair,* but it's a
fact that there are professionals (doctors, therapists,
agency directors) who don't do their jobs very well.
And, fortunately, there are those who do. You're bound
to run into some of each variety.

It was several years before I stopped *expecting*
professionals to take care of everything for me. I so
desperately wanted someone else to do it because I
felt incapable of making the right choices myself. But
it's unrealistic to expect the professionals to have all
the answers, to make all of the suggestions, or think of
all the resources. The truth is, we have to act as
partners. They need us because we know our child
best and we have learned by trial and error what
'works' and what doesn't. We need them because they
can authorize services we need, can provide an
outside perspective, and can be our advocates when
the going gets tough.

I have to keep reminding myself that professionals who work in human services got into the work because they like helping people. However, their best efforts are frequently thwarted by regulations, by lean budgets, or by slow equipment suppliers. They can't always get what we want quickly, or even *at all*, even if they *want* to. Rather than blaming them, I try to communicate my frustration with their system or their approach (remembering to have a positive attitude!). They often agree with me. Hopefully I inspire them to work towards some internal changes in the system that will benefit everyone.

Today, I will remember that taking care of my child's needs is a *team* effort and I am just as important as the professionals. Today I will write a letter that I may (or may not) send, to one of the professionals I'm having a hard time with. I will express my frustration with their attitude (scheduling, procedure, lack of sensitivity) to make them understand what it is like for me as the *parent* of this child.

"Not everything that is faced can be changed, but nothing can be changed until it is faced."
James Baldwin

I wish...

I could learn to have more patience.

Either my patience went on permanent vacation when I became a parent, or I never had much of it in the first place. Being patient and waiting is a real challenge for me, and there's a lot of *waiting* involved in special needs parenting!

I have no patience with systems (school, medical, financial aid) which seem to have built-in delays. I have no patience with equipment manufacturers who can't just box up what I want and send it immediately. I have no patience with doctors who are patronizing, or with teachers, therapists, or anyone else who won't listen to my input. I want things taken care of quickly so I can use my energy for something else. There are so many different agencies connected to our lives, that I like to keep things moving efficiently.

I *try* to have patience with people who work in various systems (often pointing out to them how their system could change). I try to have patience as I explain my viewpoint to people whose lack of experience or insight prevents them from providing the services or understanding I'm seeking. But I season my patience with a little pleasant pushiness because being patient doesn't mean giving up.

When a piece of equipment is prescribed for my son at the clinic, it usually takes a long time for any *action* to be generated. I call a few days after the clinic to remind the office staff that I am out here... waiting. I know that my son's prescription / request is sitting on a desk in a pile of other paperwork and that, unless I call attention to it, it will be waiting until it works its way to the top of someone's stack. My calls do not always get immediate results, but I like to think that they speed things up and help the agency staff connect a person with the paper. My calls make them familiar with my name and it makes me feel good to be doing something about getting my son's needs met.

Today, I will try to be patient and understanding of the agencies inefficiency and insensitivity, but I will not feel guilty about vigorously pursuing my child's best interest, and I will not give up on the system.

"You don't have to apologize for being demanding on behalf of your child."

Kate McAnaney
"How Did I Get This Tough?"

I wish...
I could maintain a positive attitude with the professionals.

I've always thought of myself as a fairly optimistic person. I tend to look on the bright side; to look for the silver lining. But my ability to be positive has been sorely tested over years of parenting a child with special needs. I know from experience that if I approach professional service providers with a positive attitude I will get much further than I will with either whining or arrogance. But sometimes I don't want to take the time to be nice and to be positive!

In some situations, with some doctors, with some therapists, with some teachers, with some IEP's, it's exhausting to keep looking for that silver lining. It's hard not to lash out to jar them into action to force a little change or initiate a process that will better serve my child's needs. In those situations, I try to count to ten, then reply steadily, "I can understand that this is an unusual situation for your school (clinic, etc.)... That it's difficult to get to all your paperwork quickly... That it's hard to imagine this plan working... But, could we take another look at this... Could you sign the authorization by tomorrow afternoon... Could we give it a try?" Parents shouldn't *have to* make more than 50% of the effort in securing services for their child, but often they do.

When we were moving from one part of the state to another, I wanted to avoid complications with schools and service providers. Rather than anticipate *resistance* in the new school district, I chose to approach it this way: I called the Director of Special Services and said, "We're moving to your town and I have a son with cerebral palsy in a wheelchair who has always attended regular classes. I'm wondering which school in your district would be most accessible for him." This initial call led to a long term positive relationship with the Director. We met before I actually moved and looked at all the schools together and chose one for Mahlon. We talked to principals and teachers. And, even though they had never had a wheelchair student in their schools before, everyone rose to the occasion and made it work.

Not all districts are this willing to make accommodations for special needs students, but I do believe that the parent's positive attitude and willingness to *help* make it work, goes a long way in establishing a worthwhile learning experience for the child *and* the adults involved. However, it's okay to let them know when you *are* frustrated. They need to be reminded of how things look and feel from *your* perspective.

Today, I will remember that my positive example will help set the tone and keep the upward momentum going in all processes.

"You have a right to believe in miracles and to make them happen."

Irving Dickman
One Miracle At A Time

I wish...

I could be a better advocate for my child. I'm so afraid to speak up.

I remember when I was a shy, inarticulate observer offering my opinion only when asked. I was the kind of person who thought of the perfect thing to say *after* the meeting or conversation was over. Assertiveness was not one of my natural talents. But that was before I had a child with a disability. It was before I had someone who needed me to be articulate and assertive.

I developed assertiveness because this kind of mothering required it. I was forced out of my shell by the necessity of defending my son's needs, protecting his rights, and procuring services for him. But my energies, both physical and emotional, are often drained by the inner battle of feeling compelled to ask for something for my son and feeling apologetic about doing it.

It isn't easy for me to be my son's advocate, but after much experience I can play the part convincingly! I'm sure the agency folks who perceive me as demanding or pushy would be astonished to find me at home crying in frustration, or agonizing over the next justification I have to make for service or equipment. Being your child's advocate takes practice and *courage.*

Today, I will list my child's needs and will realize that I am automatically justified in seeing to it that those needs are met.

"You're not a failure because you don't make it, you're a success because you try."

Susan Jeffers, PhD
Feel the Fear and Do It Anyway

Effective Parent Advocacy... The Four P's

1. POSITIVE ATTITUDE

The first thing a parent must work on is his own attitude toward his child. Parenting a child with special needs is a difficult task and everyone handles it differently. There are so many emotions involved; anger, resentment, fear, that sometimes you need a professional counselor to sort it out. Talking about your feelings can help you move beyond the tears and onto a positive approach to your predicament. Grief and sorrow have a habit of resurfacing but you can learn to control them so they don't control you. If you're feeling positive about your child and you have a positive approach to service providers, you're more likely to get the positive support you need.

2. PARTNERSHIP

Partnership with professionals is an important part of the successful advocacy formula. Although a roomful of professionals at an IEP meeting or at a medical clinic can be intimidating, you need to remember that you are the real expert on your child. You live with him and see him (or her) in many different settings so your input is essential to any decision that will be made. Consider yourself an important part of the team.

3. PATIENCE

Patience is a real challenge, especially when you're dealing with agencies which seem to have only one speed: "slow". Try to be understanding. Professionals who work in human services probably got into the work because they like helping people. However they are frequently restricted by regulations, by inadequate budgets, and by their reliance on other people for delivery of services or equipment. Communicate your frustration with their system (don't forget your positive attitude!) They may agree with you and you may inspire them to make some changes.

4. PERSISTENCE

Persistence is the last "P" because being patient doesn't mean giving up!. Parents need to follow-up on getting things they need. Don't wait for someone else to do it! The reality is, you are your child's case-manager. Make follow-up phone calls to "see how things are moving along" and to remind people that you are still out there waiting. Don't give up!

I wish...

I could feel more free and supported by all this bureaucratic assistance I'm getting!

I am infinitely grateful that there are so many assistive agencies at the federal, state and county levels for children with disabilities. I appreciate the fact that they provide so many free services to my child. But 'free' does not always feel so free. There is a hidden emotional cost for all the assistance.

I don't think service providers have any idea what a drain it is on parents to be continually subjected to the come-tell-us-all-about-yourself evaluations that are required to get or maintain services. There are intakes, reauthorizations, eligibility updates, and redeterminations. The agonizing process of assembling facts, figures, and documentation is like doing income taxes several times a year! Keeping the procedures straight is a nightmare. Some must see the child in person, others do not. Some can accept copies of documents, others want originals. Some ask you when you can come in, others tell you when to show up. It makes me want to *scream...* often.

Today, I will remember that grin-and-bear-with-it situations are common in this kind of parenting.

"Seeing ourselves as victims weakens us and impedes our healing."

Judy Tatelbaum
You Don't Have To Suffer

I wish...

I could keep other people from offering advice when they know next to nothing about our situation!

I used to feel so hurt and inadequate when someone would say something that implied that I wasn't raising my child right and that if *they* were in charge everything would be in proper order straight away. Back then I didn't have even enough confidence to feel insulted! I just assumed they were right and that I was impeding my child's progress by ignorance or incompetence. I know differently now.

I realize that no one really knows what it's like to live my life. I do my best... to stay informed about my child's condition; to address his needs with the appropriate professionals; to monitor his progress and to respect him for who he is. When people suggest that more of this or less of that would make a dramatic difference in my child's condition or progress, I politely respond, "Thank you for your interest in our life. I'll think about what you said and decide if it will work for us." I try not to get hooked emotionally by someone's well-intentioned remark. I remind myself that I am this child's parent and that I will do what I can.

Today, I will remember that a neutral or diplomatic response to well-intentioned advice will spare the advice giver's feelings and will preserve my dignity.

"Most of the trouble in this world is caused by other people who think they know better than you what is best for you."

Patrick McAnaney

I wish...

I could get break from making all these decisions.

I was a single parent when doctors suggested that my son have surgery to release the muscles in his legs. I could understand the logic of their assessment, but I had already developed a wary attitude toward any professionals who offered 'solutions' to Mahlon's cerebral palsy. So I did my homework: I got second opinions from other doctors, third opinions from physical therapists, and fourth opinions from other parents of kids with cerebral palsy. I felt as if my head would burst from trying to sort all the advice and from worry that I would make a 'wrong' decision.

Even with all that information, I was unsure. It was confusing and agonizing to have to say, "Yes, I want you to do the surgery". I wanted to cry, not decide. I'll never forget the intensity of that moment in the hospital when I had to sign on the line that gave the surgeon permission to cut my son; to permanently, irrevocably change his muscles. I cringe every time I even think about it. I hate to make decisions that may affect my child in major ways! It's such an awesome responsibility, but it is not one that I can walk away from.

Today, I will remember that there are no perfect solutions to my child's condition. Everything is a compromise, but I will always strive to get as *close* to perfect as possible.

"When you know you are doing your very best within the circumstances of your existence, applaud yourself."

Rusty Berkus
Appearances

I wish...

I could figure out whether I'm a wonder-woman or a wimp.

My friends often say, "You're amazing! I don't know how you do it" (parenting a disabled child). They look at all the extra things I have to do, like writing out my son's homework, dressing him, bathing him, taking him to the bathroom, getting him to therapy... and they see impossible tasks.

I look at my life and I see all the times that I'm too tired to finish (or even start) the homework; the times I could-but-don't bathe him; the times I'm so frustrated and impatient that I don't give a darn about his needs; the times I'm annoyed when he has to go to the bathroom when I've just sat down; and the times I *don't want* to drive him to therapy even though it's good for him. I don't *feel* like that wonder woman people think I am!

Most of the time, I'm just tired and I give myself a hard time about it. It's hard for me to see my accomplishments and to justify my exhaustion. I criticize myself for not having *more* dedication to therapy, *more* patience with teaching self-help skills, and *more* energy for the rest of the family. So when people look at my life and marvel at my courage, my strength and my patience, I want to tell them that I'm not all that courageous; I'm often impatient; and I get frustrated and lose my temper with both of my children. I want them to know that sometimes Wonder Woman feels like a wimp!

The illusion of 'saintliness' is hard to overcome. People want to believe that special needs parenting is a superhuman task because they are so sure they couldn't do it. I was certain I couldn't do it either. In fact, before Mahlon was born, I had a chat with God and suggested that he not send me a 'special child' because I surely wasn't capable enough to benefit the child! But when my premature son arrived, I just started handling it, that's all. I wasn't knighted and I didn't receive a special degree from Exceptional Parenting School. I'm just doing what I have to do with my particular circumstances. *Every* family has challenges. Just because my family's challenges are more *visible* doesn't make me a saint. There's too much responsibility in being a saint and it's too isolating to be on a hero's pedestal.

Today, I will remember to congratulate myself for all the things I do during the day, even if it is just making phone calls to service providers. I will not focus on what I should have done. I will make a list of what I do so that I can better understand where my energy goes.

"Loving the self, to me means never ever criticize ourselves for anything. Criticism locks us into the very pattern we are trying to change. Try approving of yourself and see what happens."

Louise Hay
Love Yourself, Heal Your Life

I wish...

I could separate my child from his disability for a day.

I have a long held belief that children should be given plenty of time to be children. It's their job to be children. We want them to be good at it so they can feel satisfied and comfortable moving on to the stages of adolescence and adulthood. I've observed that parents of special needs children often let the child's disability interfere with the process of *enjoying* childhood. Parents get so focused on fixing their child that an inappropriate amount of time is spent on doing things that are not *fun...* too much therapy, too many clinics, too many *goals*.

Parents need to examine their goals for their special needs children and make certain that play is high on the list. *Discovery* is what childhood is all about. There are clever ways to disguise therapy as play, but in these situations make sure you are following the *child's* lead: Don't orchestrate *all* his or her discoveries.

When Mahlon was two and was still not sitting or walking, I was trying to teach him, without much success, how to scoot himself safely off the couch so that he could crawl on the floor. My girlfriend's three year old observed my method and then quietly walked over to the couch and said, "No, like this, Mahlon." She demonstrated, rolling on her side and then sliding off the couch on her stomach. Mahlon followed suit. I stood there with my mouth open. I learned then to allow Mahlon to show me how *he* would do things.

I watched each stage my girlfriend's children were going through and tried to 'set the stage' for Mahlon to have those experiences. I would put newspapers and magazines within reach so that he could discover them for tasting and tearing. I would prop him on my knee and let him pull all the clothes out of his drawers (I couldn't resist allowing him to put them back in also!). I put him where he could smell the flowers and feel the grass. I'd like to claim that it was incredible insight and brilliance that inspired my moves, but I really think it was pride and arrogance that demanded *my* child was not going to miss experiences other children were getting! Whatever my motives, Mahlon was the winner. He is more limited now that he spends the day in a wheelchair and it's more difficult for my husband and I to carry him around, but he has a rich memory of childhood experiences to build his adolescence on.

Today, I will remember that my disabled child is a *child* first and that childhood is meant to be fun.

"We don't stop playing because we grow old; we grow old because we stop playing."
Anonymous

I wish...

I could sleep in on Sunday mornings and not have to do the same things I do all week for my child.

Everyone needs a break from routine. That's why we have weekends. Not getting to sleep in at least one day of the week seems like an infringement of basic human rights. I'm lucky because my son is bright and very verbal and sometimes he's even reasonable. I can *bribe* him to not call me until a certain time on Sunday mornings! I tried the do-this-as-a-favor-to-me routine, but it doesn't work as well as offering monetary incentives. I figure it this way: I'm paying him to *do* something for me, just as I pay my other son to do tasks for me. Staying quiet and not disturbing everyone else in the house, takes some conscious *doing* on Mahlon's part!

When he was younger and didn't understand why Mommy wasn't thrilled to come and get him up to watch cartoons at 6 a.m. on weekends, I had to just grin and bear it. I would have felt *too* guilty not getting him up. I'm not so much of a martyr anymore, but I'm still susceptible to guilt. I will sometimes shout from my bed, "I'm not coming for another half hour, Mahlon!" only to give in ten minutes later. The little voice inside me will say, "It's not fair that he has to wait for someone else to get his day started. He has plans and projects too and there he lies... waiting. How can you be so selfish, Kate." I hate that little voice. I try to remember to strike a bargain with Mahlon on Saturday nights or my husband and I decide who will sleep and who will get up. We have a system of taking turns getting him up on weekdays.

Today, I will remember that it's not selfish to want to sleep and that I will be a better parent when I'm well rested.

"To sleep perchance to dream....."

William Shakespeare

I wish...

I could get other people to treat my child like a real person.

Can you remember the number of times that someone has stopped you on the street (in the store, in the park), and spoken to your child in a patronizing, syrupy-sweet voice? Or worse, spoken to you *about* your child, without even acknowledging his or her presence? I can't count the times, but there have been enough to convince me that it's an inevitable part of special needs parenting! Since my son is older now and is verbal, we talk and laugh after such encounters. I tell my son that I didn't always feel comfortable around people with special needs and that we can't blame people for their lack of experience.

I try to educate the well-meaning masses to let them know that my son is not a 'poor little *thing*' and is not a 'crippled victim'. I try to set an example of how to relate to my son by re-directing questions to him and by using a normal tone of voice rather than baby talk when addressing him. However, I must admit, that some days or with some people I'm too impatient or too annoyed to take the time to educate. And maybe I don't always need to. Sometimes a child will refuse to be ignored, or pitied, or labeled: I remember a friend telling me that her daughter overheard a woman sigh and remark, "Oh... she's crippled." The daughter quickly corrected the woman, "I'm not crippled, I'm Nicole!"

Today, I will remember that my child and I must educate other people on how to relate to people with disabilities.

"Laughter is the shortest distance between two people."

Victor Borge

I wish...

I could figure out if mainstreaming (integration) is the right placement for my child.

You may not be able to determine if mainstreaming is the right answer for your child until you try it. For some, it opens up a whole new world, for others it's a frustrating maze. I believe that children, regardless of their disability, can always benefit from being with their 'normal' peers. Even a child severely involved with cerebral palsy who has no communication *output* can *receive* information and in his or her own way, enjoy the stimulation of a regular classroom environment. However, if your child is receiving specialized learning and therapy in a special education program and you're pleased with his or her progress, then integrating into a regular classroom may not be necessary. The end goal should be *that your child have an enriching experience.*

Successful mainstreaming is the parent's responsibility as well as the school system's. Just because there are laws that say a child has the right to the 'least restrictive environment' is no guarantee that mainstreaming will be done smoothly, effectively, or that it will be done at all. You may have to visit classrooms with your child and observe his or her level of participation. Work with school officials to determine whether placement in a regular class is appropriate. Help them recognize that academic output may not be the only measure of 'success'. There are often adjust-ments that need to be made to the quantity or the format of academic work.

An often overlooked benefit of mainstreaming special needs students is what the experience offers to the normal needs children in the classroom. Children generally don't have a problem with accepting children's disabilities as long as their questions about the disability are answered openly and honestly. I got in the habit of giving a little talk to Mahlon's class each new school year to answer those questions. And I've noticed that the other children in my son's classes have learned to be helpful, compassionate, and tolerant. And that they have often come up with modifications of tasks or games that make Mahlon's participation more meaningful. Having a special needs classmate gives children a wonderful opportunity to be resourceful.

Today, I will remember that mainstreaming is something I may have to experiment with to see if it's 'right' for my child. I will participate fully in the process of determining the appropriate placement for my child, and will remember that mainstreaming doesn't determine 'success' or 'failure'.

"To hope is to risk despair, and to try is to risk failure. But risks must be taken, because the greatest risk in life is to take no risks."

Leo Buscaglia
Living, Loving, Learning

Successful Mainstreaming

1. Talk with your child's teacher about her/his goals for your child. What are your goals for your child?

2. Observe in the classroom. Are the goals being met? Does your child seem content?

3. If you feel your child should be integrated into a regular classroom (full or part-time), talk with the teachers and administrators involved.

4. When placement is determined, observe the new classroom. Talk to the regular classroom teacher yourself. Tell her about your child, i.e. his or her personality not disability.

5. Volunteer to come talk to the entire class (with your child) to explain your child's special challenges. Let the children ask questions and answer them honestly.

6. Offer to be a classroom helper if your schedule permits.

7. Acknowledge to the teacher that you realize having a special needs child in the class is a challenge and that you will help solve any problems as they occur. Offer to go along on field trips so that your child can participate safely and without added stress to the teacher.

8. Be positive! Give other adults and children the opportunity to help. They might come up with some solutions you have not thought of.

9. Work with the teacher to establsh realistic workloads for your child. Quantities of classwork and homework may need to be adjusted.

10. Monitor your childs contentedness. Does he/she seem to be getting something out of the program?

I wish...

I could know for sure if I'm doing too much for my child.

In the morning when I'm helping my fourteen year old son put on his shirt, pants, socks and shoes, I sometimes wonder: "Who will do this for him when I'm not here? Will someone take the time? Will he find a competent, compassionate aide who won't take advantage of him? How will Mahlon manage these things?"

I've always been optimistic about Mahlon's future, but now that we're into adolescence and I know that college and independent living are not that far away, I find myself taking a harsher look at what I've done (and *not* done) for him. I question whether I've prepared him well enough to meet the challenges of this world. I worry that I've made it too easy; done too much for him. So often for *my* convenience or to stay on schedule I've hurried things along, not allowing him time to do something for himself. From his mainstream education he's gotten the social and academic skills to survive in the nondisabled world, but does he have enough 'life' skills?

Today, I will remember that there is more than one kind of 'education'. I'll encourage my child to do the things he can do for himself and I'll be patient with his efforts.

"Nothing is either good or bad, but thinking makes it so."

William Shakespeare

I wish...
I could find equipment that meets all of our needs and solves all of the problems.

I get so disappointed when a new piece of equipment only makes our life *somewhat* easier and not *a lot* easier. When we were looking for a new power wheelchair for Mahlon, I switched into my Research mode: I studied catalogs; visited equipment expos; went to showrooms; talked to other parents. Our goal was to have a powerful chair that could be used in rough terrain and that didn't tip easily. Mahlon is an active person and our home in the country has a sloping dirt driveway.

With the outrageous prices on medical equipment, we knew that the chair we chose would have to last for a long time. We finally made a selection and were convinced it was perfect. It is perfect... for *outside*. It powers up hills and it hasn't tipped over yet, but it's a monster *inside* the house! All of the doorways are battered, some of the furniture is scarred. It takes up lots of space in the house, in the van, in the classroom. The large wheels carry a large amount of dirt. The high tech computer system that makes it so maneuverable also makes it glitch out sometimes and it's confusing to repair. But... Mahlon loves it, so I know it wasn't a 'wrong' decision. It was just another one of those compromises we have to make.

Today, I will remember to keep my expectations realistic. There is no one solution to all my child's needs and my life as his parent will be full of compromises. I'll remember to be grateful that there is so much adaptive equipment available for special needs kids.

"The secret of living well is not in the answers we amass, but in the actions we take.."

Judy Tatelbaum
You Don't Have To Suffer

I wish...

*I could know how having a disabled brother is
affecting my other child's life.*

I will probably never be able to determine exactly
how my son Michael's life and personality have been
shaped by having a sibling with a disability but I'm not
sure it matters. When my sons were little and I had to
spend so much of my time helping Mahlon, I grieved
over what I felt was Michael's loss of a fair share of my
attention. I gave him as much as I had left over after
all the clinics, therapy sessions, and meetings that
were required for Mahlon. I tried to compensate by
working part-time so that I could take him to the park
or to the store while Mahlon was at school.

I noticed that he adjusted to the situation more
easily than I. His perspective was so different from
mine. What seemed a 'harsh' reality to me, was his
only reality. He did what had to be done: He modified
play so that Mahlon could be included; he
demonstrated to other children how games would be
played so that Mahlon could participate; he loaded up
the wheelchair with all the gear they needed for a
particular fantasy game and cheerfully pushed it
along. He still gets things for Mahlon and does things
for Mahlon without being asked.

Michael is Mahlon's self-appointed protector. This
became clear to me when a friend was walking with
the boys near the ocean. The friend was teasing
Mahlon by saying he would push him out to the
waves. Michael silently and deliberately repositioned

himself on the ocean side of the chair and firmly gripped the arm rest. My friend realized that this was no joke to three year old Michael. If he had to put himself between his brother and that mighty ocean, he would do it.

All in all this kind of childhood has offered Michael many opportunities. He has been able to use all of his creative talents and he's developed resourcefulness, patience, and compassion. That's not such a horrible fate. Michael may always sense that he didn't get as much hands-on attention as a young child, but I hope he will feel loved and appreciated. I always try to thank him for the things he does to help me or Mahlon. If I forget (and I do) to acknowledge his assistance, he will subtly remind me he needs a boost by asking for 'hugs'.

Today, I will remember to acknowledge the things my other child does for my child with disabilities. I will see his reality as an enriching, rather than impoverishing, experience.

"No burden is he to bear...we'll get there. And the load, doesn't weigh me down at all....... he ain't heavy, he's my brother"

Bob Russell
"He Ain't Heavy, He's my Brother"

I wish...
I could make things perfect for my child all the time.

When I read that statement and realize it holds true for *both* of my sons... the one with special needs and the one with 'normal' needs... I know I'm a pretty typical parent. Wanting Mahlon, my special needs son, to have all the advantages life can offer; to suffer none of the hurts that can be dealt; to experience joy and satisfaction, are goals for him as a *person*, not just for him because he has a disability.

We all want to orchestrate our children's lives so that they will have optimum success and minimum frustration, but each of us has our own destiny to explore, our own experiences to endure. If my mother could have spared me the pain of having lost a child, or the challenge of having a child with special needs, I would be a very different person than I am now. I wouldn't be assertive and I wouldn't have the understanding and compassion I can now offer others.

I realize, as my children get older, I have to let them accept their own challenges, learn to deal with their own frustrations, and also revel in their own successes. I will always love them and advocate for them when it's necessary, but I couldn't make their lives perfect no matter how hard I tried.

Today, I will remember that life is not perfect.

"God grant me the serenity to accept the things I cannot change, the courage to change the things I can, and the wisdom to know the difference."
Serenity Prayer
Reinhold Niebuhr

I wish...
I could make my life easier!

It's no secret that having a child with special needs dramatically changes your life. It affects your marriage, it affects your children, it affects your choices. It may determine where you live, when you work, and how you play. It means learning to do things differently and it usually takes more planning to do the things you want to do. These adjustments are often time consuming, sometimes expensive, and frequently annoying. Those are the facts. How you choose to live with those circumstances is up to you.

You don't have to allow your child's disability to *consume* your life. Parents should still pursue personal interests, take time to be alone together, and do family outings that may or may not include the disabled child. It's a tricky balance to maintain, but it's essential to the emotional health of the entire family.

My personal *stubbornness* and refusal to give up the things I like to do, has led our family to modify plans, modify equipment and *make* things work. My husband and I both love the outdoors and are avid hikers. When Mahlon was too big to carry along, we hooked the bike-buddy (bicycle cart for children) to a wide canvas belt and used it as a rickshaw for Mahlon. It also proved to be a handy place to carry the picnic lunch and the extra coats. We've used this system for mountain hikes, for walks along the beach, and for any place or time that his wheelchair is inappropriate. It does mean we have to dismantle it and transport it along in the car-top carrier on our summer camping trips in *addition* to the power chair and the manual chair (emergency backup), but it's a small price to pay for *our* freedom.

When there are activities that our other son wants to do that are really inaccessible for Mahlon (like rock climbing) we will often divide the family. One of us will take Michael rock climbing while the other takes Mahlon someplace he'd like to go. The next time we switch, so that each child has a special day with each parent. This works well for our family and insures that no one is left home not getting to do something they consider fun.

Having to continually make compromises is exhausting and often disappointing, but as tired and frustrated as I get, I really can't imagine being any other kind of parent. I think that if we *weren't* making compromises, we would not feel as close as we do as a family and we would not feel the sense of accomplish-ment that comes from getting Mahlon's needs met and desires fulfilled.

Today, I will remember that even if my life isn't easy, it is still rich with experience and opportunity and it can be fun!

"You are never given a wish without being given the power to make it come true. You may have to work for it however."

Richard Bach
Illusions

Signature On This Line, Please!

I never think I've done enough,
Despite all that I do.
Planning, organizing, moving,
All day through.

Lifting, dressing, feeding;
Then up at night time too,
To help with all the other things
My son himself can't do.

Phone calls, clinics, IEP's
Signature on this line, please!

School takes alot of time
And so much energy,
Getting in is just step one,
Much more is up to me:

Training aides and teachers,
Telling kids what's going on.
Keeping the wheelchair running...
The list goes on and on.

Phone calls, homework, IEP's
Signature on this line, please!

Then other Mom tasks still
remain,
The work is never through;
I have another son at home
Who needs attention too.

So baseball practice,
baseball games
And "Quick, Come see this trick!"
"You hold Mahlon more than me"
The guilt is laid on thick!

Phone calls, meetings, IEP's
Signature on this line, please!

Always wanting all the best,
That I can get for him;
Struggling with the agencies,
My patience wearing thin.

At evening time when I
collapse
Into my easy chair,
Before I rest and go to sleep,
A moment of despair:

Is there maybe something else
That still I didn't see?
Some new finding, some great
cure,
Some new therapy?

Phone calls, surgeries, IEP's
Signature on this line, please!

I could have/should have
rubbed his feet
For just a little while!
Worked on his computer skills,
Or dressed him with a smile!

As I let go and try to sleep,
I know one thing is true,
I'll never think I've done
enough,
Despite all that I do.

Part II:
Looking Back...

Messages from Disabled Adults

"We're different looking but not different feeling"

"My disability is only part of who I am"

"I don't think of myself as impaired"

"Disabled in body doesn't have to mean
disabled in spirit"

"We must focus on our abilities,
not our limitations"

"Let me be me!"

I wish...

...my mom knew how much I truly love her for pushing me to be all that I can be.

My mom is an amazing person. I can't imagine what she had to go through physically and emotionally to raise me. I had an older sister who was severely involved with cerebral palsy, a brother who was a premature 'blue' baby (he's okay), and a younger sister. I am moderately affected by cerebral palsy. My mom was a single parent for much of my childhood and she had to put a lot energy into pushing and prodding me through 'the system'. She was a pioneer in mainstreaming. Her philosophy was "This child has a right to go to school" and I'm sure she had to fight to make that happen. I went to a junior high that didn't even know what an I.E.P. was and to a high school that had never had a handicapped student.

My mom had to make many difficult decisions: One was to put my sister in a residential care facility. That was very hard for me because I felt very connected to my sister because of our disabilities. Another decision was to send me to a residential school for handicapped children for a year long diagnostic program. That brought up feelings of rejection and abandonment for me because my parents were getting a divorce, my sister was in out-of-home placement, and I was being 'sent away'. I wondered if I would really get to go back home. But, as an adult, I look at my 'normal' nieces and nephews and see that they also have to deal with difficult circumstances in their lives.

My mom had the same expectations of me that she did for my 'normal' siblings. We all had chores to do and, as teens, we each had to take a turn planning a meal, shopping for it, and preparing it. I hated that! In fact, I hated a lot of what I had to do then... therapy, clinics, spending summers in orthopedic surgery... but I think it helped me become the person I am. Sometimes I get depressed and I wonder if it was worth all my mom's effort? Was *I* worth it? But then the sun comes up and I know I'm definitely worth it!

I would like to say to parents: Don't ever give up on what you believe your child can do. Push him until he has the nerve to tell you to lay off.

I wish the system was more supportive of disabled adults who want to work. The system seems to be set up to sabotage self-sufficient disabled adults. There are 'gaps' that become 'traps'. I graduated from high school, I took college courses, I was trained and certified by the Coast Guard for a job, and I worked successfully at that job. However, to be entirely self-sufficient, I needed to make $15 an hour and the job paid $12. But if I make over $9 an hour, I am disqualified for the support services I need. I was caught in the middle. The Coast Guard (a government employer) couldn't make the stretch, I couldn't go without the services, so I'm not working now. But I *want* to work! Which brings me to my final message:

Disabled people are different looking, but not different feeling. We want all that anyone wants. We want to be self-sufficient. I am normal-feeling and I want to compete."

Mike Kinter
Draftsman, Oakland, CA

I wish ...

I wish I could write with my hands.
I wish I could walk down the street and not be stared at.
I wish I could cut a New York Steak.
I wish I could snow ski on two feet.
I wish I could hammer a nail into a piece of wood.
I wish I could build houses.
I wish I could meet my all time hero, Vin Scully.
I wish I could sit with Lasorda in the dugout... Tony Danza did.
   I'll pay the fine too.
I wish I could re-live the second and third weeks on July, 1982 when
   I won four gold medals in track, field, boccia, and wheelchair soccer.
I wish I could re-live the final wheelchair soccer game in which we,
   Team USA, beat Canada 2-1 to win the gold.
I wish I could enjoy reading.
I wish I could get a date easily.
I wish I could get a date with a non-disabled woman, period.
I wish I could make love twice a week.
I wish I could make love with a non-disabled woman.
I wish I could hike Half Dome with my buddy.
I wish I could play the piano.
I wish I could see the band *Genesis* three times a year.
I wish I could meet Phil Collins.
I wish I could ski six weeks a year... I "sit" ski in the snow.
I wish I could ride a bike.
I wish I could crack an egg into a pan.
I wish I could buy a house.
I wish I could complete my Master's of Public Administration program
   without writing any more papers.
I wish I could not be so serious.
I wish I could understand my parent's franticness when I fall and
   scrape my elbows.
I wish I could run a marathon with a guy I work with.
I wish I could accomplish the same amount of assignments as my co-
   workers do, in the same amount of time and with equal effort.
I wish I could have been able to handle regular school at an earlier age
   than 16.
I wish I could convince my best friend to marry me.
I wish I could play volleyball on the beach with my three ex-roomates.
I wish I could drive a stick.
I wish I could help my brother as much as he has helped me.

Craig Clifton
Financial Analyst, Los Angeles

I wish...
...I could tell the world "Let me be me!"

An adult with a disability secretly cries out to the world each day, "Let me be me!". Let me have the opportunity to do my banking in an accessible bank. Let me have the opportunity to go shopping in a supermarket without staring eyes to question my mobility. Let me have the opportunity to learn how to use a computer so I may turn on/off the appliances in my apartment independently. Let me have the opportunity to participate equally on commissions and boards in my community without prejudice from others to demean my character. I am not my disability. My disability is *part* of who I am!

When a disabled child attempts to open the door of teen years, parents show their fears of not wanting to sever the umbilical cord of parenthood. This umbilical cord represents the protectiveness from the cold, cruel, stigmatizing dragon that parents must slay to make the world a safer place for their teen with special needs. The teen on the other hand, reaches out to learn the skills for independence. Thoughts of graduating from high school, going to college, earning a living, living in one's own apartment, getting married, and experiencing the normality of raising children become highway goals on the road of life, in spite of any disability. Family support remains the foundation upon which goals are built. Successes and mistakes are interwoven into the patch quilt of one's being. Young adults need the freedom to make mistakes and create success.

I am not my disability. My disability is part of who I am.

Millicent Rogers
Senior Social Worker
United Cerebral Palsy, Hawaii

I wish...

...I could always have my physical independence.

I first became aware that I was different when I saw my reflection in a glass door and suddenly realized that I didn't walk like other kids. I asked my mother, "Why do I walk different?" She explained that it was a condition I was born with; that she and my father had blood that was different (both Rh factor) and that's why I had the condition that made me different. I looked at my differentness as 'special'. I was a poster child in the 1950's and I was made to feel very special. I didn't think of my differentness as negative.

I was born on the East Coast in 1937. By the time I was six months old, my parents could tell that something was not right. I was not behaving like a normal six month old. I had an older sister, so they knew about normal development. They took me to various pediatricians and got a variety of diagnoses. Finally they went to a doctor at a large pediatric hospital. That pediatrician told them that I would never be able to sit up or to walk and recommended that it would be 'best for the whole family' if they institutionalized me. My parents absolutely refused! Instead they got in touch with a doctor at a Shriner's Hospital and I was under his care for the first sixteen years of my life. According to my mother, I began to talk before I was one, so they knew there was nothing mentally wrong and fortunately I had no speech problems. When I was three years old, I walked.

Even though I was only slightly different than other kids, my parents had to fight when it came time for me to enter school. The superintendent was not in favor of me being in the regular classroom. He felt that I would be a burden to the teacher and would require too much extra time. The principal, however, was very supportive and finally an agreement was made for me to try it on a half-day basis. So that's how I started first grade. My mom would come and pick me up when my half-day was over. I didn't have too many negative experiences in school. My classmates were protective of me and instructed new kids not to tease me. Adolescence was hard, because I was such a terrible introvert. It's ironic that when I graduated from high school I was awarded a scholarship that was a memorial for the superintendent who had refused to let me start school! (He had died in an accident.)

I feel very fortunate to have had my parents because their goal was for me to have a normal life. They didn't want me to be dependent on them forever and they knew that dependence would not be fair to me either. So I was raised with normal expectations, chores to do and all. When I would fall (which was often), my mother would say, "Amber, get up. If you had been watching where you were going, or hadn't been hurrying you wouldn't have fallen." She was much maligned by her friends because they felt that she was too cruel to me. My mother told me years later that whenever I would fall she would get a sharp pain shooting up her right arm. She figured it was a psychological pain because she wanted so much to reach out and help me.

My mother was a ballerina and she used her extensive dance training to help me learn to fall. She put a mattress on the floor and then had me walk by her. She would suddenly trip me. I never knew when to expect the fall and I learned to relax. Even to this day it's very seldom that I hurt myself when I fall because of that early training with my mother.

I have always been very independent. I've spent most of my life as a single person and I've never regretted that fact. It has allowed me to do lots of travelling. I've been to Europe twice (once I took a group of students), and I've lived for a while in Central America. I have a Master's in Art Education and I was a teacher for 27 years. Fourteen of those years I taught on a Navajo reservation in New Mexico. I've just recently retired and fairly recently (7 years ago) got married for the first time. I'm enjoying that new experience.

As I get older, As we *all* get older, impaired or not, we tend to slow down. My biggest concern is that I'm going to be less and less independent. I'm trying to 'psych' myself up for that. I certainly don't want to become a burden to anyone. I'm finding that I have to change my attitude and let go of a little independence.

I can't walk as far or as long as I used to, so I do use a wheelchair if I'm someplace where a lot of walking is required.

I would like to have more resources on what is available to adults with disabilities. And I wish the medical community would come up with some concrete research or studies that deal with the aging process in disabled adults.

I have always been very independent.

Amber Del Vito
Retired Teacher
New Mexico

I wish...

...I could empower more disabled people.

I was born with cerebral palsy in Scott City, Kansas. My parents raised me at home so I was never institutionalized. I attended public schools in special classrooms for children with disabilities from ages four to fifteen. Then I attended a Rehabilitation Center until I was 20 years old. I went to Washburn University in Topeka, Kansas and received a degree in Communication.

All during those growing and developmental years, I had an abundance of support from my family. They treated me just like anyone else... with no pity, which is one major factor of empowerment, treating a person as a human being.

My first dream was to establish a group home for five individuals in the community while I was in college. My dad said I was nuts for even thinking of it, which made me more determined to do it! When I was 24, I became the Director of my dream home.

The purpose of the home was to allow people living there to develop their own lifestyles and to be productive and independent as much as possible. That experience reinforced my belief that controlling your own life, making your own decisions, and being responsible for those decisions is what it is all about. Everyone must realize that disabled people have *abilities*, too. We must focus on those abilities instead of limitations.

I moved from Kansas to California in 1980. My parents were not real supportive of the idea at first because it was so far away and they worried about who would help me with my needs. I said, "Don't worry, be happy!" After a dozen arguments with them, they finally supported the idea (I think!). We've had our disagreements, but they are always there if I need them.

To me, empowerment means taking control of your life, making your own decisions, speaking and acting on those decisions, taking responsibilities, believing in your values and disagreeing with your parents and other authorities.

Everyone must realize that disabled people have abilities, too. We must focus on those abilities instead of limitations.

Randy Kitch
Resource Developer, Dept. Developmental Services

Randy uses a computer with a speech-pac to communicate. He types his messages with his toe.

I wish...

...people didn't think of me as disabled.

If I had one wish, I would say I wish I didn't have it! (cerebral palsy). I am very mildly affected and I don't think of myself as impaired. I think maybe I'm an over-achiever because of it. I'm an anesthesiologist and a pediatrician. I scuba dive, play tennis and racquetball, and I've run two marathons. I always wanted to be an athlete and wonder if I could have been more of an athlete if I didn't have the cerebral palsy. But, I might not be the person I am today or may not have met the woman I fell in love with and married, if I hadn't had to deal with the challenges of being considered disabled.

There is a certain amount of trauma for any child who is labeled 'handicapped' or 'disabled'. It wasn't fun. I hated therapy. I was exempted from regular physical education in school but I didn't like the adaptive P.E. program at all. I hated being called names by other children. I had to become very thick-skinned in order not to be hurt by insensitive remarks. Unfortunately, as an adult, I find that I'm not as sensitive to other people's subtle cues (like when they are upset or angry) as I would like to be. When you have learned to ignore people when they are hurting you, you also lose sight of their signals when *they* are being hurt. Now that my wife pointed this trait out to me, I'm trying to be more aware!

I had a pediatrician when I was young who had a real impact on me. She said, "Don't say I can't. At least try!" I guess that's what I've always done.

Don't say "I can't". At least try.

Marty Clayman, M.D.
Anesthesiologist, Pediatrician
Honolulu, Hawaii

I wish...

...that more parents of disabled children recognized that feeding the soul is just as important as treating the body.

My mother always made walk to school even though walking was my greatest challenge. I fell on my face nearly everyday. Sometimes my mom would come along and help me up; sometimes I would go home crying. She would dry my tears and send me on my way again. As I left, all I saw was the confidence in her face.. that I was going to be okay; that I was going to make it. That's what started me on the road to independence. It wasn't until a few years ago that my mother shared with me, that on those days when she sent me back out the door, giving me the you-can-do-it smile, she would close the door behind me and cry. She didn't know if I *could* make it, but she was willing to let me find out.

My parents were incredible. They were the epitome of wonderful parents because they accepted my disability and ran with the challenge. My self-esteem was very important to them. They seemed to know when to work with the physical body and when to feed the soul.

In junior high, I had to wear orthopedic shoes. I love clothes and I love to be feminine and orthopedic shoes were just gross. The big thing was penny loafers and stockings. I had to wear these god-awful black and white oxfords with white ankle socks and I thought I'd die. I sat my mother down one day and said to her, "I will hate you for the rest of my life if you don't let me get penny loafers." She calmly said, "Okay, honey, let's go get them." First she had to pick me up off the floor because I couldn't believe she said yes! We went and got the shoes and I felt like a billion dollars and I proceeded to ruin my walking. But it didn't matter, because I was feeding the soul. Those shoes did wonders for my self-image. Two years later, I decided *on my own*, that it was time to get the walking under control and that walking safely and comfortably was more important than shoes. We all need those lessons. We all need to know that it's okay to fall on our faces and it's okay to make 'wrong' decisions. You've got to have those failures and those experiences so you can learn to pick yourself up, otherwise you're not going to grow as a person.

Disabled children are handled so much and each specialist deals with only a part of the body. What can happen is that the real person gets lost. Then the sense of self becomes a sense of body rather than a sense of soul. My feeling is that if you keep centered on the soul - the emotional, feeling side of yourself - the body takes care of itself whether you can walk or not. Anybody can walk, anybody can talk, and anybody can use their hands, but it's what you *feel* about yourself that gets you through life no matter what your physical capabilities.

My work as an Information Specialist on disability issues has given me the opportunity to interview many disabled adults. I have noticed that some of the most severely disabled people are out there going for it - jobs, marriage, children - even though their lives are difficult, while some people who are hardly disabled at all feel like big nothings! Obviously, it's not the disability that's the key factor in success and happiness. Self-image is the key factor. Some people had been programmed to expect everything that life had to offer and others had been programmed to think that they could *not* have all their dreams... and they believed it! Someone imposed limits on their futures. I think if you want anything badly enough, you can have it, despite any disability. I have seen it happen!

My parents always expected me to toe-the-line. They had the same expectations of me as they had of my younger brother. If you allow a disabled child to get away with inappropriate behavior just because he's disabled, you do him a disservice. I had a second grade teacher who treated me like a 'poor little crippled girl'. I did really bratty things and got away with them. I thought it was great! Then in third grade, I got a teacher who was a witch. She expected me to behave like everyone else. I can look back now and see that she was one of the people who gave me what I needed. She made me toe-the-line. When I was in high school my P.E. teacher made me try everything and I hated her for it (in a love/hate sort of way). P.E. was extremely difficult for me because it brought out all my differences and it hurt like hell to be different at that time. But she was teaching me, "Don't use your disability to limit yourself" "Don't cop out because of your disability". That lesson was a real gift to me. If teachers and parents let kids coast through school without really doing their best and if they graduate and didn't earn it, they aren't prepared for the real world.

One last suggestion I would make to parents and to professionals working with disabled children: Encourage children to enjoy the *process* of achieving a goal. I was always working towards a goal that was out there in the future somewhere. Therapy is very goal oriented. Acquiring self-help skills is very goal oriented. Children are told: "We're doing this now so that in-the-future you'll walk better or live on your own easier." They should be allowed to enjoy participating in the moment and should learn that it's okay to not reach goals all the time. My mom was super intense about therapy when I was a pre-schooler and I finally rebelled. So she had to deal with *her* feelings and learn to let go of the goals a little. I'm just learning as an adult to enjoy the small stuff; to be in-the-moment when I'm doing something. I call it 'mindfulness'. For example when I'm washing my hair I try to notice how it *feels* to have the warm water on my head instead of thinking about where I'm going to be an hour later. It's a constant challenge for me. When you can help your child (and yourself) delight in the moment, you are working on feeding the soul.

Allow your child to explore all of life. Don't limit either his experiences or his opportunities for success and failure. We all need these lessons.

Kathleen Lankasky
Information Specialist
UCPA, California
Married with two children

❖

The last of the human freedoms...
To choose one's own attitude in any set of
circumstances.

Viktor Frankl
Man's Search for Meaning

❖　　❖　　❖

When all is said and done...
"Misery is optional"

Kate Divine McAnaney

❖

References

Bach, Richard, *Illusions*, Delacorte Press, 1977.

Berkus, Rusty, *Appearances; Life is a Gift; To Heal Again;* Red Rose Press; Los Angeles, (213) 207-8211

Buscaglia, Leo, *Living, Loving, Learning;* Fawcett Columbine; New York; 1982.

Dickman, Irving, *One Miracle at a Time*, Simon and Schuster; New York, 1985.

Hay, Louise, *Love Yourself, Heal Your Life; Healing Thoughts;* Hay House; Santa Monica, CA; 1990.

Jeffers, Susan, Ph.D., *Feel the Fear, and Do It Anyway;* Fawcett Columbine; New York, 1987.

Tatelbaum, Judy, *You Don't Have to Suffer: A Handbook for Moving Beyond Life's Crises;* Harper & Row, New York, 1989.

Articles by Kate McAnaney printed in
Exceptional Parent Magazine (Subscription: 800-247-8080)

"A Camping We Will Go" March 1989

"Single Parenting: The Hardest Thing I've Ever Done" July/August 1989

"How Did I Get This Tough?" July/August 1990

Part III

EPILOGUE...

Eighteen years from the beginning

A letter to readers

Mahlon speaks out

Publisher's afterword

...and some responses from readers

Through my tears I read many of my own feelings and experiences. Your words touched me deeply and I know that I'll continue to use your book over the years.
—A California Parent

Epilogue, 1998...
A letter to readers from Kate McAnaney

Dear Friends...

My family has traveled much further down the road since the first edition of this book was published. It's been the usual journey...smooth patches interspersed with potholes that slow our progress; times to regroup and rejoice and times to moan and groan! But in the smooth patches we can see the gains we have made, and that keeps our spirits up; keeps us moving forward, even if we know there are more potholes ahead. Our lives individually and as a family continue to be challenging, but with all the pitfalls that children (and young adults) face today, dealing with the disability of a family member sometimes seems minor (other times, of course, it consumes me!)

Mahlon is now finished with three years of college. Wow! Where does the time go! As you can imagine, sending him off to live "on his own," in a community three hours away, was a wrenching experience for all of us. I had such mixed feelings. I knew I needed to let him go, but I worried constantly about who would take care of all the things that his dad and I had always done for him. Many of our worries were the same as any parent sending a child off to college: You worry about vulnerability. You worry about the adjustment of making new friends, fitting in, enjoying classes. You wonder if you've given your child the foundation he or she will need to make good decisions. But always you hope for the best.

I'm great at visualizing the best, the Ideal. I had imagined that when Mahlon went away to college he would magically be able to do all his schoolwork on his own; that he would quickly adjust to college life and love it; that the special disabled program at the college would fulfill all his needs. Meanwhile, I would be relaxing at home in my "new" life, communicating with Mahlon by phone once or twice a week, visiting on occasion. What a dreamer I was! I had "forgotten" that even if you take away the cerebral palsy, Mahlon is still a shy person who doesn't adjust quickly to change and who doesn't like to ask for help. The Reality was far from my ideal. Mahlon was terribly homesick, he hated the city, and he needed far more help keeping up with the schoolwork than any of us had anticipated. Not only did we communicate by phone several times a *day*, my husband and I commuted the three hours to the college at least once a week.

Also, in my perfect picture, I hadn't anticipated *my* emotional trauma of surrendering Mahlon's well-being to complete *strangers!* This was huge for me. Someone had to get him up in the morning and put him to bed at night. Someone had to give him a shower. Someone had to plug the wheelchair into the charger every day. Someone had to set out his books so he could study. Someone had to make sure he had all the supplies he needed. Could we possibly find attendants who were that competent and in addition were *compassionate?* I agonized over this.

Would the wheelchair withstand the rigors of long-distance driving every day? *What if* something happened and it would take us three hours to get to Mahlon? The what-if's made me a nervous wreck for several weeks. I felt like I had regressed eighteen years and was right back in the predicament of having Mahlon in the Intensive Care Nursery at Stanford and my husband home on the ranch, hours away, with me torn between the two, always anxious no matter where I was (remember the Grief Cycle? It's still here!)

I obviously had to do some letting go. Letting go...what a major issue for parents of disabled young people. How much help is enough? How much is too much? I have always struggled with this one. When and to what degree is letting go appropriate? My conclusion: Each disabled person and each family is different. I quickly realized that Mahlon wouldn't be able to cope with the challenges that college presented without a strong support system. We asked Mahlon what he wanted, he told us, and we listened. He needed the emotional support of having us come to visit often. He needed physical assistance with scheduling classes, book-buying, research and typing of term papers, and a scribe for test-taking.

I know Mahlon was teased by others his first years at college because his parents were still so involved in his life. Mahlon boldly told them that he considered himself and his parents a Team, and that was what worked for him. I was so glad to hear that! I was feeling self-conscious about being there so much ...wondering what other people were thinking about us. But being part of Mahlon's Team, by *his* choosing, makes me feel like I am doing what is right for my son, even if others are doing things differently. One thing I have learned as a parent of a disabled child is to never *assume* you know what's best for another family!

It took us all awhile to settle into a routine. Commuting to the college to help Mahlon with school assignments was well as helping him find note-takers and checking out classrooms for accessibility has become a part of our new life, but there are other new parts. With our second son off to college too, my husband and I have time to go out to dinner when we feel like it, to linger at a coffeehouse or bookstore, to sleep in on weekends. Having Mahlon away at college is maybe not what we *expected*, but we have adjusted. Life is good. We did find attendants who are competent *and* compassionate and we trusted them so much that my husband and I took a ten-day trip to Ireland on our own this year. We had a great time and Mahlon survived without us! We feel fortunate to have two great kids who are wonderful people to know. We are all happy, for the moment, and it is moment by moment that we move on, groaning a little, rejoicing a lot.

My best wishes to you and your family.

Sincerely,

Kate McAnaney

P.S. I have loved getting responses from my readers over the years. It warms me to know that my words have touched you, that my experiences have helped you in some way, that my favorite quotes have inspired you. Keep writing!

Kate McAnaney may be reached in care of the publisher, at the address in the front and back of this book.

EPILOGUE...
Mahlon speaks up

Going away to college was a major event in my life. The College part wasn't so bad, but the going away sure was! I didn't want to leave home, but I knew that I should. I could have chosen to stay home and go to the local college, but that didn't feel right. I guess I wanted to challenge myself, but it was more of a challenge than I expected! I missed my family, my familiar surroundings, and my dog. It was hard to get used to all the noise and traffic of a city since I had always lived in the country. I worried about crossing the streets and getting hit by a car. I worried that my wheelchair would break down and I would be stuck somewhere. I worried about what to do if the dorm elevator broke down. I worried what would happen to me if there was a fire in the dorm and everyone evacuated except me.

But mostly I was depressed because it finally hit me that I would always be a disabled person. I know that sounds funny but I think I was so focused on getting out of high school that I never thought about the rest of my life! I mean, I *had* thought about what I really *wanted* to do, which would be a career in the military, but I hadn't faced the fact that I would never be able to do that. I think that will always bug me. I have taken all the military history classes at my college but it's not the same as being in the military. I hate having my options limited, but I just get up in the morning and get on with my day. I deal with my disability on a day to day basis.

When I first got to college I wasn't very confident

about my ability to do things on my own. I think I adjusted pretty quickly to that. There is so much that I learned to do by computer—send messages to professors, discussion leaders and note-takers; check the online catalog for library books; sign up for services; communicate with friends by email; read interesting things on the Internet. There are still things I don't like to do, mainly asking for things I need, but I do them anyway. The best part of college (other than some of the classes) has been learning to go fun places on my own...like to bookstores and the movies. I like being able to plan what I am going to do with my day and then go do it.

Dealing with attendants has been an education. The first year I was in a program where the college provided attendant care until we hired our own attendants. That was helpful. I met lots of nice people and got used to having people other than my parents as attendants. The second year I hired an attendant who turned out to be very unreliable and that was really annoying. I probably should have fired him, but I kept giving him another chance because I'm a nice guy! This past year I had two incredibly reliable and friendly attendants. Since I could count on them, I was free to focus fully on my schoolwork.

The schoolwork is a bit of a stretch for me. I can do the reading, but I need help brainstorming for papers and putting them together. I feel that I'm in over my head sometimes. It's frustrating. At those times I ask myself, *Why am I here when it's not leading to my ultimate goal?*

Then I remind myself that my dream of being in the military is not realistic and I have to admit that if I weren't in college I don't know what else I would be doing. I feel like I am in limbo. However, I think it will be important for me to have a college education, so I'll stick with it.

I have chosen to stay in the dorm for my entire college education because it is easier and more comfortable for me to go with the *known*. Yes, the dorm food is boring. Yes, the elevator breaks down often. Yes, it's annoying when the freshmen want to stay up late and party instead of study. But I know that living in an apartment would have a whole different set of challenges and at least I'm used to handling these!

Now that I am almost through with college, I am looking at job prospects and living situations. I'm not sure what I will do. I'll deal with that when the time comes. In the mean time, I am doing some part time summer jobs in possible careers to get some ideas of employment. Since I have a passion for military history, this summer I am doing some research for the military historian at a local military base. Last summer I worked at another military installation as a library assistant.

I think it is very important to have a support system you can count on. My parents are very supportive and help me a great deal. You have to be willing to ask for help when you are disabled. You may not like it (I don't!), but it's a reality. People sometimes ask me if I have adjusted to being disabled. My answer: I don't have a choice!

I'm used to it, but I think the limitations will always be a disappointment. People ask me if I'm happy: I would say, Yes. I like who I am. I appreciate the abilities I have. I enjoy my life.

Mahlon McAnaney (May, 1998)

I borrowed I WISH... from a support group member and was so moved. It helped me be more in touch with the emotions and issues surrounding my family's special world. It helps us cope, accept and conquer.
—A Parent, New York

I think your book should be required reading for everyone with a special needs child and those who work with both the children and their parents. You have written passionately, lovingly and purposefully. You used an economy of words to convey a monumental message. You have helped me, a professional, to get inside the head of an incredibly thoughtful parent, to share her thoughts and appreciate her insights.
—Disability Organization Director, Illinois

EPILOGUE
A Word from the Publisher

For many years, Kate McAnaney's **I WISH...** has been among the most treasured books on the shelves and *in the hands* of parents with a child with a disability. Without belligerence or self-pity, this little book has had the power to bring hope, encouragement and perspective to many. This book achieves that power because its author speaks simply, plainly and eloquently from direct experience. There is a purity in this matter-of-fact witness which shows itself as well in many books which are far more widely known. But to the reader it simply means, This book can be useful.

What **I WISH...** offers isn't dogma, but wisdom that is open-ended. The process of learning and applying what has been learned is continuing...just as parenthood is. These truths are *relative* because (as Kate points out), each person and every family is different, and **I WISH...** speaks to them all.

For nearly a decade Special Needs Project has sold books about disabilities throughout the United States and the world. We are the leading source of both technical and nontechnical books for parents, educators, and all those who seek knowledge. We have occasionally published works we felt were timely and needed. Now, **Editions DSG** has been created as our publishing arm, in order to formalize this activity, making it ongoing and permanent.

When Kate and I first met, the "old" original edition of **I WISH...** was nearly exhausted. **Editions DSG** is proud to have the opportunity not only to keep in print a book we think is a classic, but to make possible this newly expanded edition. It adds an important part to the story Kate, Mahlon and Patrick McAnaney share with the rest of us: the part about *growing up*. We are delighted to bring it to you as the first "official" title under the **Editions DSG** imprint.

Hod Gray,
Director of Special Needs Project
Publisher, **Editions DSG**

There are days when I would feel that I was "crazy" if not for your book—Parent, California

I WISH... is a real gift. As grandparents of a child with special needs, it is encouraging to read a book about reality and compassion.—Grandparent, California

I cried, I laughed, I cheered! Thank you for your inspriational book.—Physical therapist, California

*Your book will be required reading for all current staff members as well as for all new employees as they go through the orientation process for our organization. I truly believe our agency will do a better job for our community after our staff has read this book.
—Service Provider, California*

(Removing this page will not harm your book)

Order Form...

I want to order Kate's book!

- copies of **I WISH...** @ $9.95	
Shipping & Handling $4 for orders under $40 / $41 up, **10%**	
Quantity discount	
Sales tax (California residents only)	
Total	

I enclose my check or money order for_____
Please charge my Visa/Mastercard.

#_____-_____-_____-_____ Exp___/____

Signature_____

Phone
(important)_____

Name
(please print)_____

Organization_____

Address_____

City,
St, Zip_____

SEND to Order Dept., **Editions DSG**
3462 State Street, #282 • Santa Barbara, CA 93105
• FAX it to us at 805-962-5087.
•ORDER by PHONE toll free at 800-333-6867
•EMAIL us— <books@specialneeds.com>
The **Special Needs Project/Editions DSG** URL
is **www.specialneeds.com**. Be sure to bookmark it.

Discounts for quantity: 10 copies, 10%; 25 copies, 20%

I WISH... is #7679 in the Special Needs Project catalog,
which offers thousands of the best books about disabilities.